Gardening
for Beginners

Contents

Introduction

Small-scale gardening

Small gardens are fun to make, and will fit in almost anywhere.

A garden can grow indoors.

A garden can grow outdoors.

All a garden needs is . . .

. . . soil or **compost**

. . . somewhere to grow

. . . plants or seeds

. . . light and water.

POTTING COMPOST

A versatile peat-based compost containing balanced nutrients and trace elements.

Busy Lizzy

Sweet pea

Nasturtium

The Sunny Seed Company

The Sunny Seed Company

Tools and things

Here are some things a gardener needs:

(1) a **trowel** *to make holes*

(2) a **garden fork** *to dig the soil*

(3) a **hand fork** *to dig up weeds and loosen the soil*

(4) a **bucket** *to carry soil, plants and weeds*

(5) a **watering can** *to water plants with*

(6) **plant pots** *for growing plants*

(7) **secateurs** *for taking cuttings*

(8) **gardening gloves** *to keep hands clean*

Secateurs are very sharp!
Make sure you have an adult with you.

Wash your hands after you have been gardening,
even if you wear gloves.

Gardening outdoors

Ideas for containers

Containers make good gardens for
small spaces, like balconies or terraces.
Here are some ideas.

Tyres make good containers for plants.

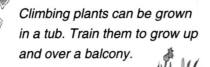

Strawberries grow well in pots.

*Climbing plants can be grown
in a tub. Train them to grow up
and over a balcony.*

Herbs grow well on a sunny windowsill.

*Lettuces and carrots can be
planted in a trough or sink.*

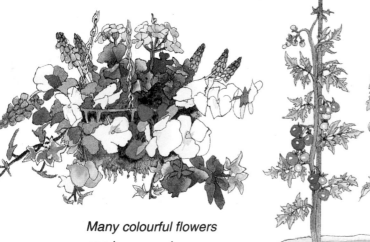

*Many colourful flowers
can be grown in a
hanging basket.*

Grow-bags make gardening easy.

*Potatoes can be grown
in a big pot.*

Choosing plants

FLOWERS

Some plants live for several years. They are called '**perennials**'.

Some plants live for only one year. They are called '**annuals**'.

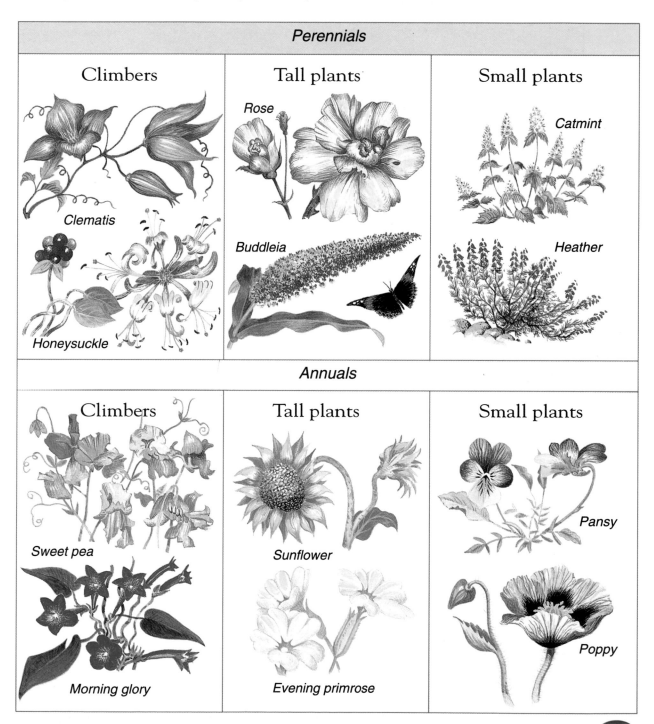

Perennials

Climbers
Clematis
Honeysuckle

Tall plants
Rose
Buddleia

Small plants
Catmint
Heather

Annuals

Climbers
Sweet pea
Morning glory

Tall plants
Sunflower
Evening primrose

Small plants
Pansy
Poppy

VEGETABLES

Vegetables are easy to grow. Most vegetables are **annuals** and they are grown from seeds. New seeds must be planted every year, in the spring or early summer.

	Need less than 6 weeks to grow	Need 6 – 8 weeks to grow	Need more than 8 weeks to grow
Roots	Radish	Turnip	Potatoes
Leaves	Lettuce	Spinach	Cabbage
Fruits and pods		Peas	Tomatoes Beans

HERBS

Fresh herbs taste delicious, especially in salads. These are **annuals**:

Parsley   Coriander   Dill

and these are **perennials**:

Chives   Sage   Thyme   Mint

WHERE TO PLANT THINGS

All plants need light. Some plants grow well only in full sun.
Others will grow well enough in the shade.

Plants that grow
well in shade:

Busy lizzie

Pansy

Plants that will grow in either
sun or shade:

Daffodil

Plants that need
lots of sun:

Rose

Nasturtium

Hollyhock

Lobelia

Evening primrose

WHEN TO PLANT THINGS

This chart shows when to plant seeds, and when to pick the flowers or vegetables. The seed packet will give more information about this.

VEGETABLES	Plant	Pick
Carrot	Mar—July	June—Oct
Garlic	Nov—Mar	June—Sept
Lettuce	Mar—Aug	May—Oct
Parsley	Mar—May	July—Sept
Pea	Mar—June	June—Sept
Potato	Mar—June	June—Sept
Radish	Apr—Aug	May—Sept
Runner bean	May—June	Aug—Oct

FLOWERS	Plant	Pick
Alyssum	Apr—May	June—Sept
Candytuft	Mar—May	June—Sept
Cornflower	Mar—May	June—Sept
Evening primrose	Mar—Apr	July—Sept
Love-in-a-mist	Mar—May	June—Aug
Marigold	Mar—May	July—Sept
Nasturtium	Apr—May	June—Sept
Night-scented stock	Mar—May	July—Aug
Poppy	Mar—May	June—Aug

Planting things

PLANTING IN A HANGING BASKET

(1) Line the basket with moss or wet newspaper.

(2) Partly fill it with **compost**.

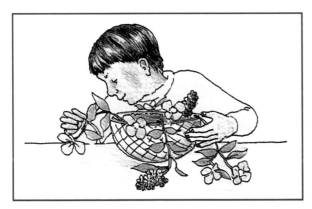

(3) Push some trailing plants in through the sides.

(4) Cover their roots with more compost.

(5) Put some more plants in the top.

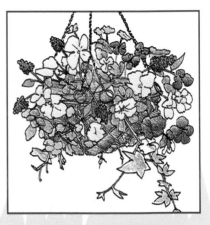

All containers, and especially hanging baskets, dry out quickly. Water them every day, or even twice a day in the summer.

PLANTING SEEDS

(1) Make a shallow **drill** (a v-shaped line in the soil) with a trowel.

(2) Put in the seeds, spacing them evenly along the drill.

(3) Cover the seeds with soil. Press the earth gently.

(4) Water the seeds well. Use a watering can with a sprinkler head on it.

(5) Put a label at the end of the row showing what seeds have been planted and when.

pansy   carrot   sunflower

The seed packet will say how deep to plant the seeds and how far apart to put them.

PLANTING BULBS

Garlic cloves are a kind of **bulb**. Plant some garlic cloves outdoors in the winter.

(1) If the garlic cloves are planted in open soil, they won't need watering.

(2) If they are planted in a container, they may need watering.

(3) In the spring, leaves will grow from the garlic cloves.

(4) By the end of June or early July, a whole new bulb of garlic will have grown from each clove. Dig the bulb up and use the cloves in cooking.

Gardeners sometimes say, "Plant garlic on the shortest day, dig it up on the longest day." Try it!

Problems in the garden

WEEDS

Unwanted plants are called **weeds**.

    Weeds grow in everybody's garden. The wind blows their seeds in, or they creep in from outside the garden.

    When weeds come into the garden, they should be pulled out. Use a fork for weeds with deep roots.

Here are some common weeds:

Plantain

Dock

Bindweed

Thistle

Ground elder

Dandelion

Couch grass

Clover

DRYING OUT

All plants need water in warm, dry weather. If their roots dry out, they will die.

Don't worry about giving them too much water. If they are in a container, the holes in the bottom will let any extra water out.

gravel

holes for drainage

If the plants are in open ground, use a watering can to soak the earth around the plants.

PESTS

Look out for these **pests:**

Aphids

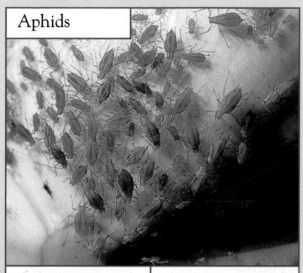

Symptoms	Treatment
Clusters of little bugs on tender shoots, buds and stems.	Wash them off with soapy water.

Caterpillars

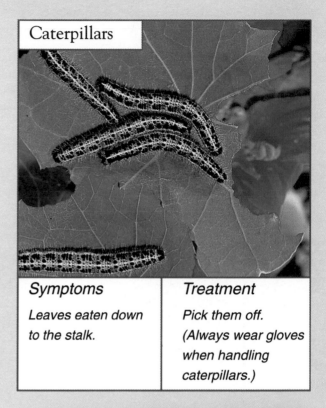

Symptoms	Treatment
Leaves eaten down to the stalk.	Pick them off. (Always wear gloves when handling caterpillars.)

Slugs and snails

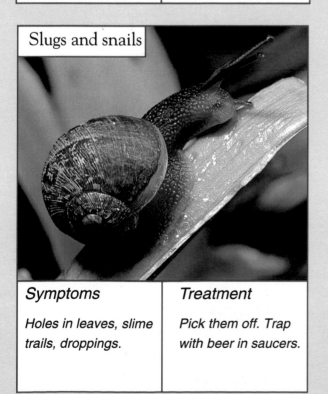

Symptoms	Treatment
Holes in leaves, slime trails, droppings.	Pick them off. Trap with beer in saucers.

Birds

Symptoms	Treatment
Seeds and seedlings pulled up.	Put thin string or netting over seedbed and plants.

Gardening indoors

Ideas to try

Many people like small-scale gardening indoors. It doesn't need a lot of space and it is very satisfying. It's possible to garden indoors all year, even in the winter.

Here are some ideas to try:

Daffodil bulb

1. Plant a **bulb**, pointed end up, in a bowl of **compost** and leave in a dark place (a garage is ideal).

2. Leave the bowl in the dark, adding water if the compost gets too dry. When the bulb has sprouted and the leaves are about 5 cm tall, bring the bowl indoors and wait for the flowers to open.

Avacodo pip

1. An avocado **pip** can take up to three months to sprout. Set it up like this.

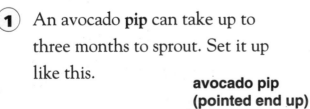

avocado pip
(pointed end up)

cocktail
stick

water

2. When it grows some roots, take it out of the jar and plant it in soil-based compost, in a flower pot.

Bean sprouts

Bean sprouts are very tasty to eat, and they are healthy too.

You will need:
    mung bean seeds
    a plastic container with a lid
    a dark place

1 Soak some mung bean seeds overnight in cold water.

2 The next day, rinse them and put them on a layer of wet cotton wool in a container.

3 Cover the container and put it in a warm, dark place, like a cupboard.

4 Every day, check that the cotton wool is damp. Water it if it is dry. Then put the container back again.

5 In about a week the bean sprouts will be about 4 cm long. Cut them and eat them, either cooked or raw.

A bottle garden

You will need:

a large transparent plastic sweet jar
   or other container with a lid
gravel
soil or **compost**
some small plants

1 Put a layer of gravel at the bottom of the container, about 2 cm deep.

2 Put some damp soil or compost on top, about 6 cm deep.

3 Make some holes in the soil and put in some small plants.

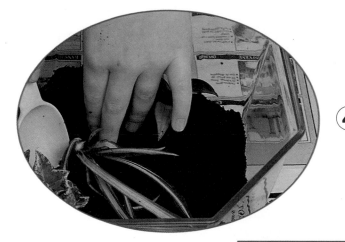

(**4**) Firm the soil around the roots.

(**5**) Put on the lid.
(You can also use
cling-film as a lid.)

(**6**) Keep the bottle garden in a light
place. Watch the plants grow.

*Never water a bottle garden. The soil will stay
damp if the lid is on tight.*

House plants

Some plants can be grown indoors in pots. They are called pot plants or house plants.

House plants can be grown from seed, but many people buy them already grown. The shop will provide instructions about how to look after them.

Good plants for taking cuttings from

geranium
begonia
Christmas cactus
busy lizzie

CUTTINGS

Many pot plants can also be grown from cuttings, like this:

(1) *Use secateurs or scissors to cut off a piece of a growing plant. Include a short piece of stem with leaves and leaf buds.*

(2) *Put it in some seed or cutting **compost**.*

(3) *Keep it watered. The cutting will grow roots.*

PLANTLETS

Grow new spider plants or mother-of-thousands plants from plantlets, like this:

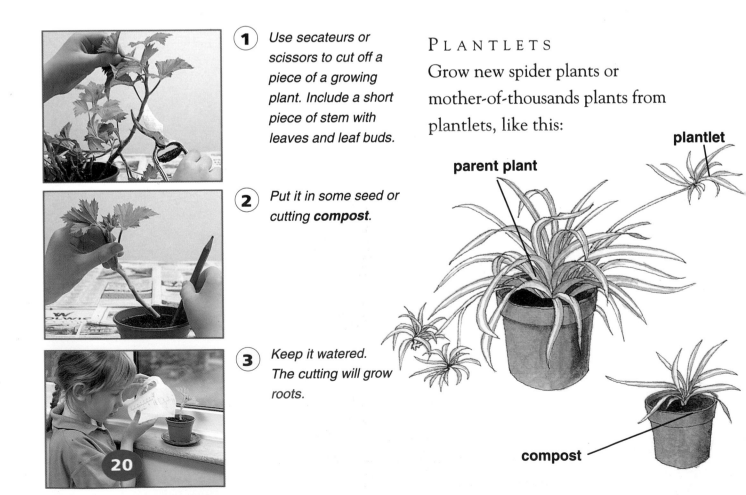

parent plant

plantlet

compost

20

GROWING HEALTHY HOUSE PLANTS

Healthy house plants need:

light

Most house plants need lots of light. If a plant goes yellow or begins to look thin and straggly, it might need more light.

water

All house plants need to be watered, but too much water will kill them. In the summer, water them two or three times a week. In the winter, water them once a week at the most.

cool temperature

Many house plants grow best in cool temperatures. Hot, dry rooms can kill them. If a plant looks sick, try putting it in a cooler place.

*More house plants are killed by over-watering than by under-watering. Never let the pot stand in water. Always let the **compost** dry out between waterings.*

RECOMMENDED HOUSE PLANTS

The plants in this list are all fairly easy to grow.

Flowering house plants

		sun/shade	cool/warm	Notes
1	**Busy lizzie**	bright, but not direct, sun	warm	Grows well from **cuttings**.
2	**Geranium**	sun	either	Grows well from cuttings.
3	**Jasmine**	sun	either	Has lots of fragrant flowers.
4	**Painted-leaf begonia**	shade	warm	Do not over-water. Grows well from cuttings.
5	**Primula**	either	cool	Do not over-water.

Leafy house plants

		sun/shade	cool/warm	Notes
6	**Ivy**	shade	cool	Keep moist at all times.
7	**Jade plant**	sun	warm	Easy to look after. Let it dry out between waterings.
8	**Spider plant**	sun	warm	Keep the soil moist.

Glossary

annual
a plant that lives for only one year

pest
an animal that harms plants

bulb
a food store for a plant, formed from swollen leaf bases, that will grow into a new plant

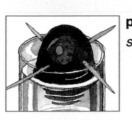
pips
seeds found inside fruits

compost
a mixture of soil and other material for planting seeds and cuttings in

plantlet
a small plant growing on a large plant

cuttings
pieces cut off a plant, which will grow into new plants

weed
an unwanted plant

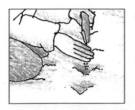
drill
a v-shaped line in the soil for planting seeds in

secateurs
special scissors that make a clean cut across a plant stem

perennial
a plant that lives for many years

Index